WRITE A BOOK IN 3 DAYS

WRITE A BOOK IN 3 DAYS

THE ZONE METHOD

MARY ANN TIPPETT

MAT BOOKS

Copyright © 2021 by Mary Ann Tippett

All rights reserved.

No part of this book may be reproduced in any form or by any electronic or mechanical means, including information storage and retrieval systems, without written permission from the author, except for the use of brief quotations in a book review.

❀ Created with Vellum

For every writer with a novel inside

CONTENTS

1.	First, A Word	1
2.	Zone In And Tune Out	5
3.	The Seed of an Idea	7
4.	Nourishing the Idea	9
5.	Deep Focus	11
6.	Outline Less	16
7.	Genres Conducive to Three-Day Novel Writing	22
8.	How to Structure A Three-Day Novel	27
9.	The Half-Book Outline	32
10.	Nail The Necessities	34
11.	Fast-Writing Fuel	36
12.	Sleep & Word-Count Goals	39
13.	Event Particulars	41
14.	Know When, Where & Why	46
15.	Support	50
16.	Anticipate Challenges	54
17.	End It Productively	60
18.	How to Stick the Landing	65
19.	Editing the Three-Day Novel	69
	Afterword	75
20.	Appendix A	77
21.	Appendix B	79
22.	Appendix C	80
	Note From Author	83
	Recommended Reading	85
	Notes	87
	Acknowledgments	93
	About the Author	95
	Also by Mary Ann Tippett	97

1
FIRST, A WORD

It has been three years since my last unfinished novel. As a former perfectionist with a list of excuses, I consider myself a member of Writing Perfectionists Anonymous.[1] Thanks to a three-day writing contest, I learned to let go of my perfectionist, story-slaying mindset and finish seven novels.

You may not be a perfectionist like me, but I would wager you have a story to tell. You have talent. You want to finish a novel. And you don't know how to get started, how to stay motivated, or what to do about that abandoned novel baby you want to finish.

You likely identify with one or more of these scenarios:

- You have a great idea for a novel and are looking for the best way to write it.

- Every time you start writing a novel, you end up quitting.
- You are writing a novel but now you are stuck.
- You have a novel in your files / box-in-the-closet / fill-in-the-blank-place-where-novels-go-to-die.
- Whenever you get into a project, you lose interest or end up chasing a new, more exciting idea.
- You wrote a chapter and now you need tips on how to write the rest of your book.
- You have a killer outline all fleshed out, but no motivation to write the actual story.
- You know how your story idea begins and ends, but you're currently procrastinating on the middle part.
- You read Stephen King's *On Writing: A Memoir of the Craft* / Anne Lamott's *Bird by Bird* / fill-in-the-blank-book-on-novel-writing and can't wait to put what you learned into action.
- You attended courses on the basics, such as outlining, character building, scene building, and the three-act structure, but when you start writing you feel like you do not know anything.
- You just do not have the time right now to commit to writing a novel.
- You do not have the credentials of a *real writer* but writing a novel is a goal.
- You read a lot of books you could have written better. Getting started is the hard part.
- You are afraid of spending years finishing a novel that goes nowhere.
- You fight with your inner critic every time you sit down to write.
- You have some partial novels to finish someday

but are too excited about a new idea to deal with them now.
- You are curious about the three-day novel process and whether it is for you.

If any of these statements resonate, you are in good company. I have suffered from all of the above: writers block, imposter syndrome, perfectionism, fear I don't really know enough yet, procrastination, time constraints, and the look-something-shiny-and-new-to-do-instead complex.[2]

But guess what? We do not need courage, years, craft books, or fancy degrees to produce our best novel. A stirring idea, a way to channel your muse, and three days will get you to the finish line.

This guide demonstrates how to write in the Zone, how to outrun your inner critic, and how to outline with the less-is-more approach. It provides a proven list of the three-day novel-writing necessities, and it shows you how to stick the landing—bringing your story idea to a productive conclusion. As a bonus, you will find that editing a novel written in the Zone is much easier than editing one that is not.

You can be one of the 3 percent who start to write a book and finish it. Three-day writing allows you to blast past the top reasons writers do not finish: procrastination, waiting for the optimal time, doubts, and writer's block.

. . .

The four sections of this book explain 1) the science of Zone method writing, 2) the minimal outlining that maximizes creativity, 3) the three-day writing essentials, and 4) how to end a novel you start and edit it into the masterpiece it is meant to be.

In short, you will learn how to:

- ZONE in and tune out.
- OUTLINE less.
- Nail the NECESSITIES.
- END your novel productively.

Let's get started.

2
ZONE IN AND TUNE OUT

"Inspiration doesn't precede action—action precedes inspiration."
—Lewis Jorstad, *The Ten Day Draft: A Writer's Guide To Finishing A Novel in 10 Days*

When I committed to writing a novel in three days, I saw it as an interesting challenge. I did not know, at the time, the oft-cited statistic that 3 percent of writers who start novels do not finish them. (I say oft-cited because no source for this statistic can be found. But judging by the number of writers I've encountered who started a novel without finishing, and by the number of writing experts who repeat this statistic, I assume 3 percent is fairly accurate.)[1] Yet I had unfinished novels in my collection. I wanted to finish one. Could I write a whole novel in three days?

. . .

Surprisingly, I could. In fact, I found the three-day writing process addictive. After writing and publishing one novel, I proceeded to write four more. When my second novel landed on the International 3-Day Novel Contest (3DN) short list, I realized not only could I finish a novel in three days, I could produce a quality novel this way.

I tried the NaNoWriMo (NaNo) approach (where writers commit to producing a fifty-thousand-word novel in a month) and came up short on word count. Instead of taking one month to finish, I brought my novel to an end in four months. The result was a mess of hastily slapped together sentences, which led to a long and painful editing process. Which is why I stick to the Zone method now.

What is it about the three-day process that works? To find out, I tracked down every book and blog I could find on writing fast. Then I interviewed eight writers, including two winners, who finished novels during 3DN.

Key to the novel-in-three-days process, I learned, is writing in the Zone.

To access the Zone, you need: (1) a spark—that seed of an idea that lodges stubbornly in your brain; (2) proper nourishment to grow the idea; and (3) deep focus to avoid the shallow ground where ideas shrivel up and die.

3
THE SEED OF AN IDEA

"There has to be a personal connection, a spark of something that you find utterly fascinating, to pull you into the story enough to need to explore it."
—Cynthia Gould, author of *Never Be Yourself* and frequent 3DN participant

The story idea, described by fast-writing author Jim Denney as "passion or intense motivation," is a compulsion to explore a topic, vision, or concept.[1]

It is that dream that wakes you in the middle of the night. That "aha" reaction you get from a TV program, tweet, podcast, quote, or conversation. That question or concept you long to explore.

3DN writers describe their spark as:

- "An image flash . . . I just couldn't shake";
- A wild story from youth;
- "An unlikable character";
- "A philosophical question, . . . what if? . . . scene that appears in my head";[2]
- And in my case, an ad on a train, a compulsion to explore a different perspective, and the desire to experiment with a new genre.

Whether you immediately jot down notes on your idea or let it marinate in your mind over time, other images and plot points will come to you. Random ideas that arise during mundane activities, like walking, dishwashing, or daydreaming, will gel around your original spark. As you feed the spark new ideas, elaborating over time, your potential story will brew. This is the start of the Zone.

4
NOURISHING THE IDEA

"I wish I felt that kind of inspiration more often. I almost never do. All I know is that if I sit there long enough, something will happen."
— Anne Lamott

Once that spark ignites, it needs encouragement. You must give it time to flourish, germinate, and evolve—time to absorb other ideas, sprouting offshoots from the original, in the days leading up to writing.

My mundane, idea-growing activity of choice is walking. While walking aimlessly one day, I came upon a dead squirrel pinned to a tree by a tiny branch. How it became lodged there baffled me. This unanswerable question fed the story idea already brewing: a novel exploring the perspective of a woman suffering from dementia. The demented mind idea I intended to explore absorbed the tethered squirrel imagery, eventually coalescing into a vivid hook—a way to open my novel and cement the theme of being stuck in a hopeless place.

This is one example of how a spark expands over time.

Whether you record the spark in some fashion or merely reflect on it, your obsession to explore that idea will feed the Zone when you start writing. But before you write your novel, you must prepare to go deep.

Deep focus is what fuels fast writing and allows you to assemble a full novel in three days.

5
DEEP FOCUS

"By pushing yourself to write quickly . . . you engage the intuitive, creative centres of your brain. You invoke the creative Muse. You invite the lightning to strike—And you tap into the miracle of writing 'in the zone.'"
—Jim Denney, *Writing in Overdrive*

The theory of flow, described by author Cal Newport in *Deep Work*, addresses how to produce at peak level. Writing at your best requires working (1) for extended periods of time; (2) with full concentration on a single task; and (3) while free from distraction.[1]

This theory, backed by neuroscientific studies, proves that intense focus strengthens neurological muscles in a manner similar to body building.

. . .

Linking the theory of flow with the law of productivity:

(Time spent) x (Intensity of focus) = High quality production

Newport explains that quality work evolves from intense focus. When you tune out everything except that nourished book idea, for a defined period of time, the quality of what you write actually improves.

Newport, a college professor, noticed most of his straight-A students spend less time studying than other high-achieving students. In his book *How to Become a Straight-A Student*, he explains their secret to success: The more efficient straight-A students carved out blocks of time to intensely focus.

Whereas some students might study in a dorm room in front of a computer, taking breaks to chat with a roommate or check social media, the time-saver A-students went to a place with no distractions to zone in on a study project. By tuning out their usual world, they minimized intensity.

As a college professor, Newport frequently produces important scholarly publications, a practice expected for career advancement. Without sacrificing valuable family time, he fulfills aggressive publication goals while meeting his professorial obligations. Publishing scholarly papers is important work, crucial to career advancement as well as fulfillment, for an academic professional. The last thing Newport wants to do is *phone in* his scholarly efforts.

. . .

To ensure the quality of output, Newport applies the law of productivity in his scheduling. Book-ending his work time with what he calls "shallow work" allows him to devote a large chunk of every day intensely focused on scholarly papers. In addition to this shallow / deep / shallow scheduling technique, Newport developed many efficiencies over time to maximize his work-life balance.

But the most important of his efficiency hacks is avoiding shallow work during deep-work time. His deep work—quality work that requires intense focus—is divided into three phases: (1) data analysis; (2) first draft writing; and (3) editing for publication. Each phase requires three to four days.

His shallow work, responsibilities which fall outside his protected distraction-free time, includes responding to emails, responding to staffing concerns, meeting with students, and making or returning phone calls. He places these shallow tasks at the beginning and end of each workday. When his workday ends, he disconnects from phone and computer, severing ties to work-related distractions.

This deep-work schedule yields impressive results, enabling Newport to publish twelve books over sixteen years. Of those twelve, *Deep Work* was a Wall Street Business Best Seller and his more recent *Digital Minimalism* is a New York Times Best Seller. While producing critically acclaimed books, he maintains his "Study Hacks" blog which attracts over three million visits a year.

How Deep Work Applies to Three-Day Novel Writing

Publishing a novel requires the same three phases Newport uses for academic output:

1. Data Analysis: Think of this in terms of any research required for a story idea.
2. First Draft: Before a book can be edited and published, you must finish the first draft.
3. Editing: Whether self-publishing or querying traditional publication sources, polishing a first draft is crucial to the novel-writing process.

Each phase takes Newport three to four days to complete. Keep in mind, these are not twenty-four hour days. These are the chunks of time that form the meat of his workday sandwich. Given the administrative and family responsibilities that flank his deep work, he arguably spends well under three full days in each phase. His ability to produce best-selling books beginning with a first draft written in three days is directly applicable to producing a quality novel in three days via the Zone method.

. . .

Among the key criteria for producing quality work, according to Newport's research, is an effective ritual. To be effective, a deep-work ritual requires:

1. A decision on the location and duration of your writing.
2. Rules designed to eliminate distractions while you are in the Zone.
3. A thought process for how to support that ritual.

The three-day novel-writing process incorporates these deep-work ritual elements. The deadline of three days plus nailing the necessities (which we will get to later), conspire to put you into the Zone and keep you there long enough to finish. Zone writing ensures your novel will be your best work.

The theory of flow demonstrates how Zone writing works. With three days to write a novel, after adequate preparation, your rapt attention to important things is ensured. Minimizing shallow work heightens the challenge, enabling a more fulfilling, focused output from your time spent writing.

6
OUTLINE LESS

"We think in story. It's hardwired in our brain. It's how we make strategic sense of the otherwise overwhelming world around us."
— Lisa Cron, *Wired for Story*

Less Is More When It Comes To Outlining A Novel

Of all the 3DN writers interviewed, few outline extensively. They typically create pseudo-outlines meant to pin down initial thoughts on how the story might go. Not only do they outline less, all end up scrapping their outlines early in the writing process.

"I wrote a very loose nine or ten bullet outline a few days before the contest," notes Dan Sanders, who generously shared his bullet points (See Appendix A). He stuck only to the first few bullet points when it came time to write his three-day award-winning novel.

"I always had an outline, although not a very detailed one," notes Geoffreyjen Edwards, Astrophysicist and regular participant of 3DN. He considers outlines to be straitjackets, adding "part of the joy of writing for me is seeing things emerge that I didn't expect, sometimes wonderful things."

Doug Diaczuk, two-time winner of 3DN, had only "rough ideas in [his] head of where [he] wanted the story to go" while writing. As for the scenes or story elements he was working toward, "for the most part [he] reached them, though not all the time."

Departing from the plan is a common theme echoed by Cynthia Gould, author of *Never Be Yourself: You're Better Than That* and regular 3DN contestant. Her outlines vary from detailed to a few scribbles. Still, she admits "things usually go off the rails pretty quickly."

"My outline for *The Second Detective* was really bare-bones," two-time 3DN winner Shannon Mullally shared in a 2020 interview. "It was a list of numbered scenes that would mention which potential character or characters would be in the scene." Predictably, she did not stick to the plan. "I didn't follow the outline during the contest. I don't remember referring to it again after I made it."[1]

. . .

For a 3DN, outlining is merely a way to picture the story in your head. Once the contest begins and the Zone is activated, something near magical happens that enables the story to spill out organically.

Jim Denney, a proponent of fast writing, zeroes in on the magic that happens while writing a novel via the Zone method: "Spontaneity is one of the joys of existence, especially if you prepare for it in advance."[2] Preparedness does not so much come from plotting out a story in detail; rather, it arises as your spark of an idea sprouts wings during the pre-writing nourishment stage.

Mullally understood this connection between attempts to outline and writing in the Zone. Scenes and character notes she committed to paper "helped get [her] subconscious chewing on it and working on possibilities and permutations before the contest," she suspects. "Because when I started writing, the story poured out of me."[3]

Stephen King said, "Stories are found things, like fossils in the ground."[4] The Zone takes you to the archaeological site of your story and digs up the details one after another. To ride the Zone wave, you expect the story to pour out of you and have faith in the process.

When Mullally speaks of her subconscious chewing on the ideas she jots down, she encapsulates a phenomenon Alex Pang identifies in his book, *Shorter*.

. . .

Recent work in neuroscience and the psychology of creativity shows that our brains actually keep working on problems when we turn our attention elsewhere, and that scheduling rest periods after intensive work gives us time to recharge our batteries while allowing our creative subconscious to continue searching for solutions to problems that have eluded our conscious effort.[5]

In other words, conscious problem-solving stays alive in our subconscious long after we hang up our work hats.

Advocating for shorter workdays, as hundreds of companies in the world have embraced, Pang maintains that important work happens when unnecessary distractions are removed. Compressing work periods into smaller amounts of time naturally requires the minimizing of shallow tasks, which in turn optimizes quality performance.

Pang's work observes that when employees have more time off work, their productivity level improves. Why? Because their subconscious is free to problem-solve outside of their shortened work-focused time periods. "Rest, as it turns out, is not work's competitor; it is work's partner."[6]

Three-day novel outlining is a means for consciously summarizing the story idea. When it is time to write, your subconscious finishes the job.

You Intuitively Know What Makes a Good Story

"Plot grows out of character."
— Anne Lamott

As author and story coach Lisa Cron points out in a podcast interview,[7] the number one mistake most novel writers make is believing that plot and flowery writing are crucial to storytelling. A good novel is not about plot. It is about your character. Your protagonist, and that character's misbelief, are the most important parts of novel writing.[8]

"Outlining the plot before you develop your protagonist traps you on the surface of your novel—that is, in the external events that happen."[9] The plot is not what keeps a reader's interest. How the protagonist responds to events and why is what keeps a reader engaged.

"The best preparation for writing any story is to know with clarity what your protagonist's worldview is, and more to the point, where and why it's off base. Thus you have a clear view of the world as your protagonist sees it and insight into how she therefore interprets, and reacts to, everything that happens to her. It's what allows you to construct a plot that forces her to reevaluate what she was so damn sure was true when the story began. That is what your story is really about, and what readers stay up long past bedtime to find out."[10]

If you think about every good book you have ever read or movie you have ever watched, the plot was nothing more than a boilerplate genre into which your favourite character was plunked. Plot "is just a series of events that happen in a story . . . Then you add in a character who needs to change and does change by the end."[11]

Although many three-day novelists believe you must pick either plot or character when preparing to write, the debate is meaningless. A compelling character with a misbelief is instrumental to the unravelling of events in your story. Character drives the plot.

7
GENRES CONDUCIVE TO THREE-DAY NOVEL WRITING

"A formula can be a great way to get started. And it feels so great to finally dive into the water; maybe you splash around and flail for a while, but at least you're in."
— Anne Lamott

Story genres (or the templates into which your characters are dropped) come with expected word counts. Literary fiction averages seventy to ninety thousand words. A person can type, write, or dictate only so many words in three days. Ninety thousand words are not in the three-day writer's wheelhouse. 3DN organizers suggest aiming for thirty thousand words (about one hundred double-spaced, typed pages).[1]

Thankfully, there are some fun genres that typically max out at fifty thousand words. Let's examine the character-first concept with respect to genres most conducive to three-day writing. The following story types provide an ideal template in which to place your protagonist.

The Quest

In a quest story, your character wants something and is sent on a journey with obstacles in pursuit of it. Laura Roberts, author and three-day novelist, recommends a hero's quest format to avoid getting bogged down in plot issues.

"Lots of writers get hung up on plotting because they don't know where their story is going. Hopefully if you've got a clear enough one-liner to describe your story, you can keep asking yourself how the characters will accomplish that goal, and you'll be able to see your way out of any jams."[2]

As an example of Roberts's point, consider Dorothy, a well-known quest pursuer in *The Wizard of Oz.* She wants to get home to Kansas. Her quest is to steal the broom of a particular witch to trade with the wizard for her return home. How will she accomplish this goal? After the good witch gives her the coveted ruby slippers, what does Dorothy do next? Who does she meet along her (yellow brick road) journey? Each element of the story boils down to the question: what does the heroine do next?

Conflict propels a story. The hero, or heroine, and sidekicks she meets along the way, will battle through a myriad of obstacles to get the object of her quest. If you have done the work of understanding your main character and what she wants, including her misbelief, when you launch her on a journey with conflicts and obstacles, she will eventually discover her misbelieved truth was keeping her from getting what she wants all along.

To illustrate using an actual three-day novel, consider Clara from *Clara & Pig*. In my first 3DN entry, the main character thinks escaping her senior home and returning to her former residence will make her happy. She does not want to get to know people in her new surroundings because she believes when you get close to someone, they leave. By the end of the novel, Clara has bonded with two people who prove their devotion to her by offering to join her quest. She now knows not everyone leaves, and that her misbelief made her lonely and miserable.

In between Clara and her goal of escaping are conflict and obstacles that provide tension: someone tries to run over her dog, she breaks residence rules that turn people against her, she gets lost and runs out of gas . . . The hero's quest story practically writes itself once you know your character and what she wants. Throw her a conflict, then ask, "What will she do next?"

The Romance

The romance story formula is simple: two people meet, fall in love, break up, then get back together. Romance readers expect a happy-ever-after ending. Sub-genre romance stories, such as comedy, paranormal, and erotic, average forty thousand to one hundred thousand words, making the story you plunk your love-starved character into writable in three days.[3]

The Murder Mystery

Many mystery stories, especially the cozy genre, tend toward lower word counts than literary fiction. Although basic plot points must be thought through in a mystery, such as how the murder happens and who did it, the main character can easily drive the plot forward based on a misbelief. For example, your *Murder, She Wrote*-style amateur sleuth suspects something which, after a perilous close call, turns out to be wrong.

Exploratory or Experimental Genres

A great thing about three-day novel writing is it provides a safe zone for blending genres or trying out a genre you are not used to writing. A hero on a murder quest falls in love on his journey—why not? Sci-fi villains band together to rid the world of romance? Anything is possible when you start with a character who wants something and carries along a misbelief.

General Fiction, As Opposed to Nonfiction

Most three-day novelists agree that writing nonfiction or historical fiction is tough to pull off in three days.

"Nonfiction would be trickier, since you need to research, and follow a logical path. With fiction, you can just slam a coffee and see what happens," notes Gould, three-day novelist and author of *Never Be Yourself: You're Better Than That*.

. . .

"Maybe not something that would require a ton of research" was Sanders's response to the three-day-friendly-genres question. "I would think you'd want to limit your trips into the real world."

"It is a 'novel' contest, so fiction is key," concludes Brenton Dickieson.

I side with these three-day novel writers on trickiness of nonfiction, having learned the hard way with my lacklustre attempt to write historical fiction about a ghost ship in three days. Though fictional, the story required research on the historical time period and players in a factual tragedy. It was the shortest 3DN novel I ever submitted, requiring so much editing I have all but given up on fixing it. But feel free to prove me wrong (see "Experimental Genres" above).

Whichever genre you choose for exploring your idea, the story will take on a path of its own once the Zone kicks in. As Diaczuk explains, "A character can always take a drastic left turn and the plot will follow," noting the inefficacy of "trying to stick to a rigid story arc."[4]

8
HOW TO STRUCTURE A THREE-DAY NOVEL

"Everyone I know flails around, kvetching and growing despondent, on the way to finding a plot and structure that work."
— Anne Lamott

Most three-day novelists aim for a minimum of thirty thousand words. This word count makes goal planning easier. Write ten thousand or more words each day, and you will have yourself a novel by the end of Day Three.

To ensure Day One is productive, I like to establish a hook and compelling scene. For *Clara & Pig*, it was Clara and her dog coming upon the dead squirrel in a tree. For *Pairs with Pinot*, it was Faith being given a deadline to find a job or fall in love before eviction. For *Murder at The Penny Lane Book Club*, it was the scene of the crime where a key character is found dead. After writing the opening scene and hook, my mission to provide non-stop action and conflict would take over, keeping the pages turning.

The structure, in other words, is hook and compelling first scene plus piles of conflict and action.

As you think through your minimalistic outline, jot down ideas on hook, opening scene, sources of conflict, obstacles, and where you see the story ending. Some scene ideas will come from fixed genre-dictated pieces (a dead body or a meet-cute, for example). As you nourish the idea over the weeks leading up to writing day, let your mind ruminate over set pieces, obstacles, and conflict sources—jotting down whatever you think needs remembering.

Every three-day novelist approaches structure differently. I have used various approaches to organize my thoughts into a rudimentary outline. For *Clara*, I sketched out key characters my main character would encounter. For *Pinot*, I had a twenty-six-question guide on love to frame the back-and-forth perspectives of my love interests. For *Murder*, I tried out a mind map technique to come up with scene ideas. Other outlining ideas to explore as you attempt to harness story parts are the snowflake method, outline in reverse, fifteen beats, and the three-act structure.[1]

I highly recommend reading Jessica Brody's *Save the Cat! Writes a Novel: The Last Book on Novel Writing You'll Ever Need*, which explains the fifteen beats of every story.

Honestly, no other book on writing I have read makes storytelling clearer than Brody.

In the end, it won't matter which structure technique you employ for pulling together a loose outline. That piece of paper will be dropped like a hot potato when the Zone kicks in, sending your character off to the races.

That said, three important points are worth mentioning before leaving the structure topic.

Think in Three Acts

Making some attempt to understand the three-act structure will go a long way toward shaping your story once you start writing.

Act One: Introduce your protagonist, describe his everyday life, and provide an inciting incident as close to the beginning as possible. The tornado in *The Wizard of Oz* was an inciting incident, for example.

Act Two: Describe the upside-down world your character is suddenly thrust into due to the inciting incident (like the land of Oz). This is the middle part of the book where your protagonist leaves his comfortable way of life and an uncomfortable one takes over. Here you will create confrontation, obstacles, and complications for the protagonist until he eventually learns his lesson (that his misbelief was wrong).

. . .

Act Three: The resolution, you will lead up to a climax and begin to resolve questions raised along the character's journey. You will wrap up loose strands and provide an explanation for them ("Oh! Dorothy had the power to go home all along by clicking her ruby-red shoes. She just had some lessons to learn before that could happen").

The beauty of using a three-act structure is you can divide your time over the three days of writing into ten-thousand-word increments each day (one act each day). Noel Alcoba, two-time finalist in 3DN and winner of WriteFighters 3-Day Novella Contest, specifically mentions his allegiance to the three-act structure when he outlines and writes three-day novels.

Read Books and Pay Attention

Reading books you enjoy will automatically shape the way you tell a story. As I said in the beginning, you already know what makes a good story. It's in your DNA. And if you don't trust this as gospel, reread one of your favourite books right before the contest to refresh your subconscious awareness of what makes a good story.

Structuring Tricks

Come up with a creative trick to weave your story around if you can.

. . .

Sanders divided his 3DN winning novel *The Loop* into the present (where his protagonist is wandering through a purgatorial loop) and the past (various scenes of the protagonist's life that shed light on his experience in the Loop). Referring to his setting as "a time-shifty afterlife," he found "whenever I got stuck in one setting, I could switch gears to another point in the character's life, or another section of the afterlife, and it wouldn't break the story. Being able to pivot like that helps. If you're stuck in one place, move on to another place."[2]

For my short-listed novel, *Pairs with Pinot*,[3] I framed the two love interests' perspectives around their answers to a soulmate app questionnaire. Using a study I found, where two strangers discussed a list of twenty-six questions designed to create intimacy between them, I knew I had those twenty-six questions to keep the plot going. Each chapter began with the characters' answers to a question. This structure enabled me to pivot from one character to another when I got stuck.

If you can come up with a structuring trick, like Sanders's past vs. present lives or my twenty-six questions, if you have a favourite book fresh in your mind, or if you can envision the three stages through which your story will lead the protagonist, you will be well prepared for the Zone to do its work when it's time to write.

9

THE HALF-BOOK OUTLINE

"I figured out, over and over, point A, where the chapter began, and point B, where it ended, and what needed to happen to get my people from A to B."
— Anne Lamott

Having had the opportunity to participate in meet-the-author chats through my affiliation with an Instagram book club, I noticed some of my favourite authors who are pantsers—meaning, they do not outline their books ahead of time as plotters do—write a partial outline toward the end of their writing process.

This jogged my memory. Once you set a character on a journey riddled with conflict and obstacles, she will eventually make choices you didn't expect. Naturally, whatever ending you envisioned will either change or require a different path. This happens in most of my novels during the three days of writing. At some point in those three days, I start outlining a few chapters ahead of the current one to ensure I don't leave out anything critical on my sprint to the end.

Though it's important to start the three days with a *plantser* approach (minimal outline), by the time you pants your way toward the end, you may turn into a last-minute plotter to get your character across the finish line. I call this a half-book outline because, like the traditionally published authors mentioned, a book can start off pantsed and become plotted partway through. (See Appendix B.)

10

NAIL THE NECESSITIES

"Time constraints are a funny thing. Even as early as our school days, we always operate with better focus when we have time constraints."
—Josh Long, "How I Wrote a Book in 3 Days"[1]

Finishing a novel in three days entails some preparation outside of spark-nurturing and story structuring. You have to find three days to write, decide on a location for writing, and dream up an incentive. The stakes for completing your novel must be compelling or the odds of finishing are slim.

Preparing yourself involves the following considerations. You will encounter energy crashes without some consideration for fuel and sleep. You may need support to withdraw for three days. Ask yourself what must happen, if anything, to ensure a three-day absence from ordinary life is doable. Lastly, expect challenges. Knowing the issues other three-day novelists encounter will allow you to anticipate problems and strategize how to navigate around them.

Hence there are five essentials you will need going into three days of writing: fuel, sleep, event particulars, support, and coping strategies.

11
FAST-WRITING FUEL

"Not to get all hippie-dippy on you here, but I honestly believe that you are what you eat, and if you put garbage into your body, you will get garbage out."
—Laura Roberts

Novelists interviewed took one of three approaches to food during the contest: planner, laissez-faire, and hybrid. While planners thought through their menu, and laissez-faire types had no plan, those in between did a bit of both.

The laissez-faire writers foraged from motel vending machines, ordered pizza, had snacks on hand with rough ideas for meals, or made spontaneous decisions about food.

Planners stocked up on frozen food and sandwiches, drank lots of water, stuck with their usual meal routines, and/or created a menu in advance that included meals and snacks.

They were mostly junk-food dodgers, other than one person who saved a pint of Ben & Jerry's as an end-of-contest reward (an approach I highly respect).

As for the part-plan, part-wing-it contestants, when asked about food planning one said, "Not this year. Maybe I should." And the other started his multiple three-day novel stints with the same McDonald's meal each year, eating when and what his family ate thereafter.

Personally, I like to feel my best going into the three-day writing scuttle. I get so excited as the day approaches, I cut back on alcohol, stick to my usual fitness schedule as much as possible, and choose healthy, nourishing foods over junk—all to save me from browbeating myself during the contest over avoidable energy issues.

Speaking my language, three-day novelist blogger Sean Di Lizio wanted to avoid "battl[ing] against sleep deprivation, sugar highs and lows, mood swings and headaches."[1]

Having meals planned out saves my in-the-Zone brain from lapsing into decision-making mode. And just as importantly, having planned, spaced-out meal breaks gives me something to look forward to, essentially breaking up my writing time into manageable chunks.

. . .

Here is my tried-and-true meal plan: two takeout dinners divided in half (chicken stir fry and rice, and a small veggie pizza); coffee, banana bread, and a peach for breakfasts; veggie bean chili and an apple for lunches; low-sugar, high-protein bars for snacks (chocolate peanut butter is my favourite); and two glasses of water with every meal plus flavoured soda water to make hydration interesting. I make the banana bread without sugar and with extra protein to avoid fatigue from sugar crashes. (See Appendix C.)

If you lean toward planner mode, Laura Roberts provides pages and pages of quick and nourishing suggestions to ponder, from frozen foods to takeout.[2]

If you are inclined toward laissez-faire mode, no judgment, but God be with you.

Some writers have support in the food provision department, relieving them from the fuel-planning burden. If you don't have the luxury of a live-in chef, I highly recommend giving some forethought to stocking food essentials before the contest.

12

SLEEP & WORD-COUNT GOALS

"There is a time for many words, and there is also a time for sleep."
—Homer

When I first read about the 3DN, I imagined writers checked into a hotel or gathered in a library to scrawl or type day and night until 12:01 Tuesday morning (the contest takes place over Labour Day weekend—convenient for people who are off work on Monday).

Now I know going without sleep is a bad strategy.

The how-much-and-when-to-sleep question is linked to word-count goals. Generally, one double-spaced, typed page has two hundred fifty to three hundred words. Whereas a fifty-five thousand word novel equals approximately two hundred pages, the more-realistic-for-three-day-writers novel length (thirty thousand words) roughly equates to sixty pages. If you have your words-per-day novel length in mind, you can set sleep goals around it. Structuring sleep around your word-count goals helps propel fast writing while protecting restorative sleep.

What do each of the three days look like?

13

EVENT PARTICULARS

> "I survived ... and wrote a book to tell the tale!"
> — Laura Roberts

<u>Day One</u>

I find Day One of writing to be particularly challenging. Although my goal is always ten thousand words or more, I often fall short.

All but one of the three-day novelists interviewed achieve higher Day-One word counts, writing 32 to 42 percent of their novels that day, according to the daily word counts they shared with me.

<u>Day Two</u>

Day Two is usually more productive for me, maxing out at twenty thousand words or more.

. . .

3DN organizers predict "this is . . . the day that the outline . . . [is] discarded." What I call the Zone, the organizers refer to as a "malevolent unleashed force that, in effect, takes over the driving."[1]

"I once 'came to' in the middle of the living room floor," admits Gould, "with the fan torn apart, cleaning the blades. I have no idea why I decided that it must be cleaned right then. I have no recollection of when I stopped writing, or how I got there. My brain must have short circuited."

One possible explanation for Gould's experience relates to sleep deprivation. Studies note a lack of focus sets in after seventy-two hours of staying awake. Persons in this state "can face some weird experiences . . . [such as] hallucinations, tremors, false memories and muscle aches."[2]

Other contestants mention bouts of tears, sadness, and laughter. Sanders acknowledges being emotional when he writes. "If I'm writing something and I'm discovering the world as I write it, I almost always get a rush from it."

Weird things happen on the second day. Sleep-related euphoria begins to colour your experience as word-count-chasing ramps up.

Day Three

Day Three is a sprint to the finish for me. I learned from

year one that I can type at the rate of one thousand words per hour when necessary. This knowledge enables me to calculate how many words are possible on Day Three, a useful number to know when it comes time to tying up loose ends—a necessary step toward bringing the story to its conclusion.

Unlike me, most of the contestants experienced a writing taper over the three days: writing the bulk of the story on Day One, less on Day Two, and fewer words on Day Three. Almost everyone made time to read over their stories, scanning for obvious errors to fix, before the midnight deadline. A couple of us incorporated basic editing into our day-to-day writing schedule.

Contest organizers advise against editing as you write. Zone theory seems to support that advice, suggesting that editing invites your inner critic and pops you out of the Zone.

My approach to save editing time in the final hours of the contest is to review the last few pages or paragraphs each time I sit down to write after a break. To avoid popping out of the Zone, I correct only obvious errors like typos and punctuation.

My mission in this periodic rereading is obvious or minor error correction and reacquainting myself with where I left off in the story. I do not second-guess what I have written. It is a quick scan only—meant to jog my memory and get on with the writing. It is not an opportunity to rethink anything critical. Rethinking would throw off my Zone-channelling focus.

Odds are, sleep will be compromised substantially by Day Three. Structuring sleep around writing goals is the ideal approach to ensuring both things happen: sleep and writing. But inevitably, you will be writing in the Zone when you should be sleeping.

Count on lingering sleep deprivation effects after the contest. The longer you go without sleep, the more compromised you become from a cognitive impairment perspective. Consider this little nugget from sleep science: Twenty-four hours of sleep deprivation is the same as having a blood-alcohol level above the legal driving limit.[3]

One hour of sleep deprivation can cause car accidents. Fatal car accidents spike every year when clocks move forward for daylight savings time, which is largely attributed to "sleep deprivation and misalignment of the drivers' circadian sleep rhythms."[4] If fatal accidents increase after a one-hour sleep loss, imagine the effect that diminished sleep over three days would cause.

Every year, I am surprised how loopy I feel by the third day of writing and how exhausted I am in the days and weeks that follow. Now I realize those few hours of lost sleep over the weekend can't be replenished in one night of make-up sleep.

According to experts, it takes four days to recover from just one hour of sleep loss.[5]

Diaczuk had a similar experience to my post-contest loopiness. "What did surprise me was just how mentally, emotionally and physically drained I was at the end of the three days. But that was accompanied by an incredible sense of accomplishment, so it balanced out."

How the three days unfold relates to sleep and goal setting. Set word-count goals. Structure sleep around those goals. Expect sleep to suffer. Oh, and don't drive sleep-drunk after the contest.

Day One may be frustrating or productive. Day Two is all about riding the Zone. And Day Three will be a typing sprint or an opportunity to edit, depending on how Days One and Two go.

14
KNOW WHEN, WHERE & WHY

"Chaining yourself to a keyboard for three days . . . teaches discipline. Sometimes you need to put your head down and work. Happiness occurs when you accomplish goals."
—Cynthia Gould

Now that you have your fuelling and sleep needs sorted out, give some thought to where to write, when to write, and how to stay motivated to write.

Louis Robert Stevenson, one of several notable fast-writing authors, wrote (the second version of his first draft of) *The Strange Case of Dr. Jekyll and Mr. Hyde* in three days.[1] Inspired by a dream, Stevenson's story poured out of him. He wrote behind closed doors in his seaside home, with minimal interruptions by his wife.

While Stevenson's writing was spurred on by a dream, there are other ways to incentivize three-day writing.

. . .

Fast writer Jim Denney uses word-count or chapter goals to keep him on task. "If you want to produce writing that is compelling, drenched in emotion, and crackling with energy, then set a goal for yourself: 'I won't break for lunch until I reach 2,000 words,' or, 'I won't sleep until I finish this chapter.'" He is in good company. Famed author John Steinbeck, who finished *The Grapes of Wrath* in five months, wrote in his journal: "When I am all done I shall relax, but not until then. My life isn't very long and I must get one good book written before it ends."[2]

Setting a date may provide all the incentive you need. If you commit to three days on your calendar, notify key people of your unreachability during those three days, and come up with a plan for sleeping and eating, you have essentially made an announcement witnessed by others. Others who might be cheering for you or counting on you to be done with it so they can see you again. Family or roommates are potential witnesses to your floundering, should you decide to quit. Ramifications like these from date-setting can certainly propel you through three days of writing.

Location can be an incentive as well. Will you write in your home office with the door closed? Will you check into a hotel for three days to write? Booking a hotel adds an expense that might raise the stakes for finishing. J.K. Rowling purportedly checked herself into a lavish hotel to finish the last instalment of her Harry Potter series.[3] She knew the longer she stayed, the greater the cost. A double incentive for getting the work done.

Perhaps you own a cabin in the woods, or you know a friend who does. The calming influence of nature might be all you need to stay motivated.

Surprisingly, most three-day novelists interviewed wrote their novels at home or in familiar surroundings. Familiarity provides access to supportive things like a kitchen, a comfortable bed, and perhaps people willing to fight off well-meaning interrupters.

Sanders learned the hard way that a motel is not always a good idea. He and his family were planning to spend the week at a familiar beach house located hours from home. His plan was to check into a motel on the way, write his novel, and join his family on the beach after the three days. "I spent one night there, then left the next morning and finished writing in the beach house . . . It was a little weird to get to the vacation and immediately lock myself away, but everyone understood." Not only did he find the motel unappealing, the only available food sources nearby were Domino's and a vending machine. "I hate Domino's," he said.

For Sanders, the support of family, agreeable food, and a familiar location were crucial. Even if it cost him seven hours of writing time. "All my non-writing free time over the weekend was devoted to driving [from the motel to the beach house]." Setting a date and location for your writing goes hand in hand with motivation.

For me, nothing is more motivating than registering for 3DN. The registration fee and the deadline for submitting my novel are powerful incentives. Even when I considered giving up, thinking about my post-contest disappointment always brought me back to the laptop. I pictured that deadline passing and me with no entry to submit. How would I feel? I didn't want to know.

3DN is only one of two contests that currently provides this three-day-novel writing challenge. If this sounds like a powerful incentive for you, consider looking into 3DN at 3daynovel.com and the "3-Day Novella" writing contest at writefighters.com. Most of the three-day novelists interviewed encountered temptations to quit. That they stuck with it shows what a strong incentive a deadline-plus-fee contest can provide.

The resolve to finish a novel in three days is motivating in itself. It has challenge written all over it. And being able to say "I finished my novel" at the end of three days is its own reward. Someone once said, "Give your story a life." It's a mantra I repeat often during the three days of writing.

Make sure the stakes are high enough to motivate getting the deed done. "Only those who dare to accept a bold and risky challenge will experience the joy of creative 'flow.'"[4]

15
SUPPORT

"Ask your loved ones to help you out on your journey before plunging them straight into the heart of darkness and barking orders at them."
—Laura Roberts

When I committed to entering 3DN that first year, I was nervous. Though I rarely make Labour Day weekend plans, the contest does take place over a holiday. Extracting myself from the family (two grown sons, a husband, and a dog—at the time) seemed like a selfish decision. But I had been waiting for years to be in a place where I might feel comfortable taking on the preposterous challenge of three-day-novel writing. Getting my husband on board with that decision was priority number one.

Though he looked at me like I might be in a manic midlife-crisis phase of life (and, fair enough), he eventually realized I was serious, and he got on board. Once I cleared that conversation hurdle, and the household agreed to my no-interruptions and pet-care-delegation requests, I knew I was home free.

To underscore the fortuitous importance of my husband-on-board hurdle, an electrical experiment gone wrong caught fire over that first three-day writing weekend, which prompted some quick thinking and acting on his part. Writing through the shrieking, pulsating fire alarm was not ideal. But being part of the debacle problem-solving would have been a major in-the-Zone buzz-kill.

Perhaps you live alone or have greater confidence in your family's self-sufficiency skills. Either way, an important part of three-day-novel planning is figuring out what supports to have in place to protect your writing time and mental health.

Laura Roberts, who lived alone when she entered the contest, decided she would need a caretaker. "Just ask your spouse or parent or friends to make sure you've got enough to eat and to check in regularly to see if you've taken your vitamins or need any special items at the store while you're in the throes of the madness that is the three-day novel-a-thon," she suggests.[1]

Knowing your social needs will help you decide on caretaker appointing. Some people have no problem spending three days without human contact. Others might gain some therapeutic reassurance from limited engagement with friends or family mid-contest.

"I let people know months ahead that [any social commitments] is a no-weekend possibility for me. And then I use those people to cheer me on in social media," three-day novel contestant Brenton Dickieson shares. "My family is key to my success," he goes on to explain, noting their willingness to make meals and go on about their business without him.

Other than updates on social media, most of the contestants spurn all social interactions, some warning friends and family ahead of time. Many contestants appreciate the get-out-of-social-obligations-free pass. "It's a great excuse to avoid all people for some quality alone time," Gould points out.

Whether you are a socialite or hermit, be prepared for unexpected social yearnings to crop up. One year, Diaczuk recalls, "I was struggling the second day, so a friend offered to meet up for a bite to eat and chat about the problems I was having. That probably took away a few hours of writing time, but it kept me going and if I hadn't done that, I probably would have quit."

"One year I had a party that had been booked months ahead of time," notes 3DN contestant Edwards. "I decided it wouldn't hurt to take the time out to change my headspace. I left early, but it was good for me."

...

Given Diaczuk's and Edwards's experience, having a caretaker on standby as Roberts advises is something to consider.

16
ANTICIPATE CHALLENGES

"Chaining yourself to the keyboard for three days straight is weird and unnatural. Wrists and necks get stiff, you overload on caffeine and carbs, and things get mental."
—Cynthia Gould

A key component of Zone writing is blasting past some writer-specific challenges. Although you will be writing quickly, there will probably be stretches of time where you feel stuck. "Burnout is the bane of writers."[1]

If you anticipate burnout with a coping plan, you will be back into the Zone swing before you know it. "You might go for a run, or hang out with your dog. Maybe you call a close friend, or perhaps you sketch in your notebook," Jorstad writes in *How to Write a Novel in Only Ten Days*. "Whatever your outlet is, make sure it's something that helps you zone out and relax. You don't want your outlet to be distracting like

TV or the internet because the goal is to let your mind work through any subconscious blocks it may be experiencing."[2]

"But one of the necessary preconditions to entering 'the zone' is a state of being physically relaxed, emotionally calm, and mentally alert," according to fast writer Denney.[3]

One way to reengage the relaxation element that brings you back into the Zone is exercise. Though some three-day novelists made time to run, most could not spare that much time away, opting instead for short walking breaks and stretching.

"Stretching is crucial!" remarks Gould. "A quick walk around the block is great for waking you up and clearing your head."

"I plan in time for a walk once or twice a day," notes three-day novel writer B.D. Wilson.

"If I was feeling particularly restless, I might have taken a quick walk to clear my head," Diaczuk says, adding he does not plan for exercise.

As for me, I learned the first year when the fire alarm went off and I was forced outside for a few minutes that a quick walk break goes a long way toward clearing my head and releasing some kinks in the muscles. Now, I fit in at least one walk-about during the three days. And I keep my yoga mat open on the floor for impromptu stretching.

There is a reason why the act of walking restores the writing brain. Cal Newport explains, in his discussion of options for supporting deep work, that affording the conscious brain time to rest allows the necessary shift for the unconscious brain to sort through difficult challenges. He references a 2008 study that validated attention restoration theory, noting that walks in nature restore attention fatigue and provide boosts in concentration.[4]

Alex Pang makes a similar observation in his book The Distraction Addiction, referencing a Latin phrase attributed to ancient philosophers, *solvitur amulando*, meaning "it is solved by walking."

"I have walked myself into my best thoughts," Kierkegaard declared. Nietzsche agreed, saying, "All great thoughts are conceived while walking." Pang explains how walking resets the creative mind: "Restorative activities and environments occupy your conscious mind, leaving your unconscious free to work without deliberate effort and with an understanding that the pressure isn't on as much."[5]

As for those stiff wrists and necks, think what coaches tell their athletes who experience pain in the sport. "Walk it off."

. . .

One challenge I noticed in myself is the tendency to feel discouraged on Day Two of writing. In year one, I felt like I was writing the most boring chapters ever as I tried to connect the Act One action to the Act Three wrap-up. In year two, I was plunged yet again into that muddled middle despair, floundering for ways to keep the action interesting while my broken-up lovers were adjusting to not being together. In year three, my characters were literally at sea, as was I, trying to create action and drama on a ship caught between its berth and its mysterious abandonment.

Last year seemed more optimistic at the start: I had a more detailed outline, which kept my mind active, looking for places to insert key plot points in my murder mystery experiment. Even so, I was ready to give up completely on Day Two, in fact walking away with that intention. There is something mentally exhausting for me to be in that in-between place while I'm writing.

Perhaps what I was experiencing is the discomfort that comes from committing to something that is hard. Forcing myself to stay with a story with only quick kitchen trips to break up the writing tedium is grating. The thrill of finishing a novel, a goal I was lucky to achieve even once, lost its lustre during the tedious in-between moments of writing.

But a funny thing happened when I gave up on Day Two last year. Walking away released my brain from the commitment to finish. I was okay with it. I could finish the story on my own time, I decided. By Day Three, however, I understood that walking away meant losing touch with the story that is ever-present in my mind when I am writing in the Zone. I would lose the continuity that Zone writing provides. I would have to familiarize myself with the plot and characters all over again. And I would only be putting off the discomfort I was feeling for later.

I would be in that same in-between tough spot, lacking a deadline to catapult me through it. I realized how much I needed that deadline to bring my novel in for a landing. So I woke up on Day Three, did a quick assessment of how many hours were left, set a new word-count goal, and typed like a house on fire until the deed was done. I believe that the relaxation I experienced with my decision to walk away on Day Two reinvigorated my resolve to get back to work on Day Three.

Many of the challenges expressed by three-day novel finishers mimic the same challenges experienced when writing a novel over a longer period of time: self-doubts, a place to focus, mental and physical fatigue, and emotional highs and lows. The only difference is that the three-day deadline forces a persevering attitude that raises the stakes of quitting.

Preparing for the inevitable highs and lows going into the three days gives you the tools to blast past those challenges in a protected—dare I say—magical space. One of those tools is permission to literally walk away until you get back into that relaxed, creative zone.

. . .

Perhaps Gould's time on the floor taking apart her fan gave her brain a similar reinvigoration experience, enabling her to work more productively thereafter.

And Sanders's seven hours of driving during the contest to escape a crappy motel did not hurt the quality of his creative output. Perhaps the break was more necessary than he realized, given his entry took first place.

17

END IT PRODUCTIVELY

"You can't edit a blank page."
—Jodi Picoult

Interestingly, only two of the 3DN finishers interviewed had finished novels prior to the contest. The others found their stride through 3DN writing.

Sanders: "I don't think I could say I ever gave it a real honest shot. I've done NaNo a few times . . . but I don't know if my NaNo novels would qualify as earnest attempts to write a novel."

Annie Mahoney: "I've written novels before, never quite finished or edited. Without a deadline, I'm sloppy and unfocused and things don't go well. I outline then get bogged down in the outline. 3DN works for me."

. . .

Edwards: "The first time I did this, I had written but not completed several novels."

Noel Alcoba: "I tried for years. I'd get as far as four chapters. But 99% of the time it was pretty much just writing and rewriting the first chapter."

Gould never attempted novel writing before 3DN. Although she was short-listed for the award one year, she considers the contest a writing exercise. She now writes novels and novellas for a living. "It trained me how to write fast, and trust my instincts . . . It's boot camp for writers of all kinds!"

As for me, I started and abandoned several novel attempts, the only exception being one I co-wrote with a friend for fun that now gathers dust in my place-where-novels-go-to-die. 3DN works for me. NaNo, on the other hand, has not been particularly helpful. After researching and using the Zone method, I now understand why.

Quality, Not Quantity, Brings A Novel To Completion
"Quality is more important than quantity. One home run is much better than two doubles."
—Steve Jobs

The NaNo objective is to finish a fifty-thousand-word novel in thirty days. If you stick to the organized procedure, your word count each day of November is logged onto the NaNo website. Thirty days seems like a lot of time, but it's actually not. To complete fifty thousand words, you need to average between one and two thousand words per day. Almost all NaNo writers wedge their writing time into their daily routines.

Writing this way—stealing time from ordinary life to sneak in one to two thousand words toward a novel—naturally twists the novel-writing goal into a word-count-focused rather than a story-continuity-focused objective. Creating a readable story falls to the wayside as word count takes over.

For example, local NaNo affiliated groups organize write-in sessions where writers can be in the company of other writers. Leaders of the Write-Ins run writing sprints where a timer is set for twenty minutes and writers in the room type as quickly as possible during those twenty minutes to see how many words they can get down on a page. Prizes are awarded for the highest word counts at the end of the timed sessions. The advantage of this technique is it teaches you to write without overthinking. The disadvantage is the resulting words are largely useless.

When I finally finished the one novel I started during NaNo (three months later), I was bored to death with my story. The spark that inspired it was long gone. Even worse, I now had a huge chunk of writing that needed to be cut and honed. Editing was drudgery.

All of my 3DN novels were comparatively fun to write and easy to edit. Getting in the Zone unleashed a mysterious ability to bring my spark of an idea to a satisfactory ending. People say writing is hard work. And it is. But does that mean it has to be torture? If you enjoy writing enough to write a novel, shouldn't it be fun, at least a little?

Most 3DN novelists agree that nonfiction is not amenable to three-day writing. Nonfiction is not a novel, for one thing. It involves research and time in the real world. This book you are reading now is a work of nonfiction. I left no stone unturned, no blog unprinted, no book on fast writing unread in my quest to uncover the reasons three-day novel writing works. Armed with a binder full of highlighted research and a detailed outline, I decided to give NaNo another try for completing a first draft of this book.

Well, folks, the quantitative vortex of NaNo took over my objectives yet again. After the first few pages, I resorted to data dumping to meet my word-count goals each day. Copying and pasting chunks of my research into ill-conceived outline categories was the only way to get through the process. Although I finished a first draft in thirty days, I basically had a slightly more organized outline of research points. The words I used to connect the points were meandering and tentative. Just like my first NaNo novel, I ended up rewriting it from scratch. Because my NaNo books were not written in the Zone, I had a hot mess of words with no readable narrative weaving those words together.

Statistically, NaNo finishers have an unimpressive track record for publication. Nearly a half million writers have won

NaNo over the years (winning is logging in fifty thousand words in thirty days). Of the half million novels, two hundred fifty entries have been traditionally published. The percentage of NaNo winners to NaNo publishers, in other words, is about 0.05 percent.[1]

Why so few? Because NaNo incentivizes quantity—word count—over story. 3DN, on the other hand, incentivizes quality—a readable novel—over word count.

Statistics are scarce on 3DN finishers over the forty-three years of the contest. In 2020, over two hundred fifty writers took part in the contest. But every year since the start, the organizers publish a winning novel. Prior to announcing the winners each year, a short list of at least three finalist novels is announced. This means that judges over the forty-three years deemed at least four hundred thirty-three 3DN novel entries worth publishing. Over four hundred readable, award-worthy novels! And these were all first drafts.

Three-day writing, in other words, enables you to produce a readable novel from beginning to end. It may not be fifty thousand words, but every word will count.

18

HOW TO STICK THE LANDING

"You don't need to know exactly how the story is going to end, but you do need to know what the protagonist will have to learn along the way."
—Lisa Cron

Regardless of how you end your novel, the single driving force of starting is bringing your main character to the end of her story. To use a technical term, the hero's character arc must be completed.

"Your lead character should be centre stage at the end. Everything he learned throughout all the complications that arose from his trying to fix the terrible trouble you plunged him into should by now have made him the person who rises to the occasion."[1]

Your ending should close out the emotional roller coaster you put your reader through.[2]

. . .

Certain genres dictate their endings. The couple must be together and on their way to happily ever after in a romantic comedy. The murderer must be identified along with the weapon of choice in a murder mystery. But regardless of the story type, the main character dictates the novel's ending.

In the typical three-act structure, remember, the hero starts out living his everyday life, doing what he does. Then something happens (a catalyst) that catapults him into a different life. He will spend all of Act Two trying to pursue his goal in this new upside-down life, harbouring a misbelief about the world as he scrambles over the hurdles you throw at him. By Act Three, he understands where he went wrong. He has a new perspective on life, and whether he accomplished what he set out to do or not, he is a different guy from the Act One guy.

Whether or not you are knowledgeable on plotting, your story comes from a place that resonates with you. When you explore that place during 3DN, the hero starts to call the shots. She may be driving toward the ending you imagined. Or she may end up in a whole new place. But the process, in a Zone-fuelled space, unravels naturally.

For me, the reality of 3DN endings is driven by a clock ticking down while loose ends remain flapping in the wind. I am in the middle of my story, typing at a rate of a thousand words per hour, and I realize I have to bring it in for a landing before the clock runs out. At the very least, I need to *Scooby-Doo* unresolved plot points (unmask the villain, throw that couple into a warm embrace, uncover the smoking gun). But the story will end. Otherwise, I cannot submit at the contest deadline.

Here are some examples of what not to do, if possible, as the story wrap-up begins:

1. Tack on the cliché it-was-all-a-dream finale.
2. Invent a rescue out of nowhere like lightening striking to kill the villain in the nick of time.
3. Provide no resolution, where your hero spent the novel striving for something and in the end leaves the quest undone for no reason.[3]

If you cannot think of a good twist, a happily ever after, or a lesson-learned ending idea, you can bring the story full circle, where everything comes back to the beginning scenes.[4]

Without knowing full circle is a thing, I resorted to this type of ending with my first 3DN. My hero was in a hopeless place at the start of the novel. And by the end, she was in the same hopeless place, albeit with new friends who seemed to like her. How did I know to use this type of ending? The same way you will.

Read books and pay attention to how the plots of books you love unfold and end. Even if you do not pay attention, you will have internalized the essentials of a good ending. And by the time you have ushered your main character through a Zone-fuelled series of disasters and triumphs, you will know where it is all leading. Trust me on this.

You can tell yourself no matter what ending you tack on, you can always change it later. If that gets you to the finish, by all means, do that. In my experience, when I go back to reread my novel after a long break, I find the ending is exactly right. Whether or not my readers will agree, I am always satisfied the end suits the journey. This is how a novel gets finished. You write it in the Zone, bring it home for a landing, and ignore all those temptations to tweak, rewrite, or scrap the whole project.

Give your story a life.

19
EDITING THE THREE-DAY NOVEL

"So the writer that breeds more words than he needs, is
making a chore for the reader who reads."
—Dr. Seuss

Because your three-day novel will be written under deadline, in the Zone, after months of incubating your idea, the story will be naturally bare-bones. You may have thrown in the odd eloquent verbiage or meandering paragraph, but the overall sense of the novel will be a compact story with continuity and purpose. It will be a complete thing, almost living and breathing.

Unlike the editing of novels written over weeks, months, or years, three-day novels are easier to edit. The multiple steps that go into editing a larger manuscript are, for the large part, not necessary.

. . .

Sanders puts it this way: "The editing process is pretty light. There wasn't really much to it. The way to think about it is: edits are for the reader rather than for the story. So it's more about [smoothing] out the rough edges than adding an entirely new section or something like that."

To paraphrase Ian Cannon, the steps for editing a typical novel are:

1. Print and read the manuscript, making edits and comments about the story (what is missing, what should be removed or added).
2. Rewrite the novel, incorporating said comments.
3. Print and reread, making more comments that pop up on story issues.
4. Rewrite again, focusing on language and whether the sentences are the best possible.
5. Print and read the novel aloud, making edits on the page as you do so. Then fix what your edits suggest needs fixing.
6. Do a final, checklist-based edit.[1]

Compare these six steps (and other experts have longer lists than Cannon) with editing a three-day novel, which are:

1. Do a final, checklist-based edit.

That's right. Unless you are unhappy with your story for whatever reason, you can mostly skip all that printing, rereading, rewriting business.

There are exceptions. For example, the historical fiction novel I attempted one year was well under the thirty thousand word count I aimed for. Rereading revealed areas where the story needed more explanation, more backstory, and more clarification on whether the main character is a ghost or a person. But historical fiction is steeped in nonfiction. Writing it requires months of research and detailed outlining. And as mentioned under the genres section, nonfiction is not ideal for three-day novel writing.

It is possible upon rereading you might discover a gaping plot hole that undoes your wrap-up. Say, your protagonist could not have been in the same room with the victim because he was out of the country during the time of murder. This type of problem will require more than a checklist-based edit. I have not seen this happen, likely because the continuity aspect of Zone writing naturally prevents plot holes. But if you are loopy enough, you could miss something critical.

These are the only exceptions I can think of, because when you write in the Zone, your plot stays fresh in your head and gaping holes are nearly impossible.

All of my three-day novels required a checklist-based self-edit before turning them over to a professional editor to polish. In one case, I added an epilogue based on pre-publication beta readers' feedback: they wanted to know more about my rom-com couple after they came together at the end, which I thought was fair. I wanted to know too. Still, the novel ending stood on its own without the epilogue. Given it was short-listed for the 3DN award, no additions were technically necessary as far as the judges were concerned.

The point is, my three-day novels required no major additions or rewrites. Clarifying language was added. But nothing that required multiple print-outs and rewriting of substantial storylines. There will be no storyline issues in most cases. Sentence clean-up and grammar or typo corrections can be penned onto one printout.

Contrast this one-printout editing process with NaNo books. I have printed, corrected, printed again, rewritten substantial parts, changed point of view, tried summarizing key points to rewrite once again, condensed long meandering portions into smaller ones, printed again and corrected again. These multiple steps happened with both my NaNo novel and this how-to guide (the first draft of which I put together during NaNo). Three-day novel writing, in my experience, eliminates most of those steps, requiring merely a checklist-based self-edit.

What is involved in a final, checklist-based self-edit? You can read Cannon's blog for details, but generally you will be looking for grammar, typos, inconsistencies, places you can cut, words you use too often, and whatever else sticks out or bothers you.[2]

If you intend to self-publish or prepare your manuscript for querying traditional publishers, you should hire a professional editor after your checklist-based edit. Professional editors simply know more about what to look for in a seamless manuscript. But you will need a copy edit only (the cheaper of all the professional edit options usually).

This minimal edit feature is the best-kept secret of three-day novel writing. A huge advantage to writing a novel in three days is that the concise, well-formed, completed story you churn out will be easier to edit. Hands down.

And easier to read. Dr. Seuss might even say: a writer who breeds only the words that he needs is making a novel that's more fun to read.

AFTERWORD

"There should have been a better farewell. But in the end, there never is. And we take what meagre scraps we can find."
—Richard K. Morgan

Thank you for coming along on my how-to-write-a-three-day-novel journey. If you are now considering writing a novel in the Zone, I have fulfilled my purpose. I have written novels both ways—in the Zone and over long periods of time—and frankly, three-day writing is more fun. It beats back all those doubts and excuses that commonly crop up for writers. And it unleashes the freedom to pour out a story creatively and completely.

Although the three days of writing has its challenging moments, typing the end to a readable story brings a sense of accomplishment unlike any other. All it takes is getting into the Zone, creating the tiniest of outlines, attending to necessities for getting through the three days, and sticking the landing.

As Longfellow said, "Great is the art of beginning, but greater is the art of ending."

THE END

20

APPENDIX A

Minimal Bullet-Point Outline Created by Dan Sanders for 3DN Winning Novel *The Loop*

Ch. 1
Just the walk. The set up. I don't know where I am. A man appears.

Ch. 2
Can't talk to the man. Can't look at the man. More people. The horizon bends.

Ch. 3
My father appears. I am permitted a scream. This chunk should suggest that he's been in the loop for a very long time. The scene bleeds into past.

. . .

Ch. 4

Addict as addict, as repetitious failure. Round things. A wheel.

Ch. 5

Interventional experience. Echoes on the horizon. Father is alive, helping. Over and over, helping.

Ch. 6

Maintaining the mistake, diggin in. Blames his father. He runs his father over, hustling away from help. Shifts back to loop. He returns to whatever addiction and is later arrested.

Ch. 7

A clearing with a single tree, surrounded by other, smaller trees. The scene in your head. There is a man, it does not matter who, they don't know each other. They talk about life. About the loop. About where they are and what it is. You are dead. You killed your father and hung yourself in prison.

Ch. 8

We are allowed to see the loop straighten. It leads to the mountain in one direction and to the beginning in the other and we are left at the centre, the sky above, milky way spiralling in either direction.

21

APPENDIX B

Half-Book Outline (Written on Back of Minimal Outline) For 3DN Entry *Clara & Pig*

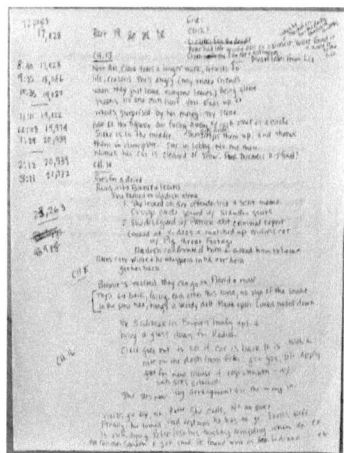

22
APPENDIX C

All Energy No Sugar Banana Bread Recipe[1]

- 1/2 C. Almond Flour
- 1/2 C. Coconut Flour
- 1 Tbsp. Tapioca Starch
- 1 1/4 tsp. Baking Soda
- 1/2 tsp. Salt
- 1/2 tsp. Vanilla Extract
- 2 Tbsp. Coconut Oil
- 4 Eggs
- 3 Ripe Bananas
- 1/3 C. Cacao Nibs

Preheat oven to 350 F. Spray 9" x 5" loaf pan with cooking oil spray or use coconut oil.

In mixer, blend bananas until liquid. Then add vanilla and coconut oil. Mix well.

Add dry ingredients next, stirring slowly in mixer, then folding with a spatula.

Fold in cacao nibs. Dump the mixture into the loaf pan.

Cook for 40-45 minutes. Let cool, and voila! (When cool, I slide knife around the edges to loosen, then turn the pan over to plop the loaf onto the cutting board.)

NOTE FROM AUTHOR

Word of mouth is crucial for any author to succeed. If you enjoyed the book, please leave a review online. Even if it's just a sentence or two. It would make all the difference and would be very much appreciated.

Thanks!
　Mary Ann

RECOMMENDED READING

Recommended Reading

Although many of the sources cited in this book elucidated Zone writing for me, I found the following sources particularly instructive.

On Writing In General:

Jessica Brody, *Save The Cat! Writes A Novel: The Last Book on Novel Writing You'll Ever Need* (Ten Speed Press, 2018)

Ian Cannon, "A 7-Step Process To Editing Your First Novel Into Print | Everything You Need To Know About Editing Novels," 2019, **https://www.thisisallcanon.com/blog/everything-you-need-know-about-editing-novels?rq=editing**

Stephen King, *On Writing: A Memoir of the Craft* (Scribner, 2010)

Recommended Reading

Ann Lamott, *Bird by Bird: Some Instructions on Writing and Life* (Anchor Books, 1994)

"6 Ways to Outline Your Novel," WildMind Creative for Authors, 2020, **https://wildmindcreative.com/bookmarketing/6-ways-to-outline-your-novel**

On Writing In The Zone

Jim Denney, *Writing in Overdrive: Write Faster, Write Freely, Write Brilliantly* (Second ebook Edition, 2013)

Cal Newport, *Deep Work* (Grand Central Publishing, 2016)

NOTES

1. First, A Word

1. Not a real thing.
2. Real things.

2. Zone In And Tune Out

1. K.T. Anglehart, "97% of Writers Don't Finish Their Novels: 5 Steps to Be Part of the 3% and Write a Book in 10 Months," Polished Pages, 2018 https://www.polished-pages.com/post/write-a-book-in-10-months.
   Lorraine Santoli, "The Top Reason People Never Finish Writing Their Book," The Synergy Whisperer, 2015 https://thesynergyexpert.com/2015/10/20/the-top-reason-people-never-finish-writing-their-book/#:~:text=Did%20you%20know%20that%2097,30%20actually%20complete%20the%20task.

3. The Seed of an Idea

1. Jim Denney, *Writing in Overdrive: Write Faster, Write Freely, Write Brilliantly*, (Second ebook Edition, 2013), 59.
2. Dan Sanders, Annie Mahoney, Doug Diaczuk, and Brenton Dickieson respectively in discussion with the author, 2020.

5. Deep Focus

1. Cal Newport, *Deep Work* (Grand Central Publishing, 2016). 84, 97-98

6. Outline Less

1. "A Q&A With 2017 Winner Shannon Mullally," 3-Day Novel Contest, Published Dec. 17, 2020, https://www.3daynovel.com/2020/12/17/a-qa-with-2017-winner-shannon-mullally/.

2. Denney, *Writing in Overdrive*, 29.
3. "A Q&A With 2017 Winner Shannon Mullally."
4. Stephen King, *On Writing: A Memoir of the Craft* (Scribner, 2010), 163.
5. Alex Soojung-Kim Pang, *Shorter* (Public Affairs, 2020), 13-14.
6. Pang, *Shorter*, 14.
7. Lisa Cron, interview by Bianca Marais, "The Biggest Mistake Writers Make: Lisa Cron," *The Shit No One Tells You About Writing* (Season 1, Episode 8, 2020).
8. Lisa Cron, "The Biggest Mistake Writers Make."
9. Lisa Cron, *Story Genius: How to Use Brain Science to Go Beyond Outlining and Write a Riveting Novel (Before You Waste Three Years Writing 327 Pages That Go Nowhere)* (Ten Speed Press, 2016).
10. Lisa Cron, *Wired For Story: The Writer's Guide to Using Brain Science to Hook Readers from the Very First Sentence* (Ten Speed Press, 2012).
11. Jessica Brody, *Save The Cat! Writes A Novel: The Last Book on Novel Writing You'll Ever Need* (Ten Speed Press, 2018), 3.

7. Genres Conducive to Three-Day Novel Writing

1. "Rules," 3-Day Novel, https://www.3daynovel.com/rules/.
2. Laura Roberts, *Confessions of a 3-Day Novelist: How to Write an Entire Book in Just 72 Hours* (Buttontapper Press, 2014), Kindle loc 192.
3. Blake Atwood, *A Word Count Guide for 18 Genres, Including Novels and Non-Fiction* (The Write Life, 2020).
4. Doug Diaczuk in discussion with the author, 2020.

8. How to Structure A Three-Day Novel

1. "6 Ways to Outline Your Novel," Wild Mind for Authors, 2020, https://wildmindcreative.com/bookmarketing/6-ways-to-outline-your-novel.
2. Dan Sanders, "AMA about writing a book as quickly as you can type or any other possibly bad ideas," Reddit, Aug. 29, 2000.
3. Originally entitled *The Chipmunk, The Sommelier & Fishing for Souls*.

Notes

10. Nail The Necessities

1. https://blog.teamtreehouse.com/how-i-wrote-a-book-in-3-days

11. Fast-Writing Fuel

1. Sean Di Lizio, "A Novel in Three Days," The Millions, Last modified August 25, 2020, https://themillions.com/2010/08/a-novel-in-three-days.html.
2. Roberts, *Confessions*, Kindle loc 250-356.

13. Event Particulars

1. "Survival Guide #7," 3-Day Novel Contest, https://www.3daynovel.com/survival-guide-where-you-should-be/.
2. Carly Vandergriendt, "How Long Can You Go Without Sleep? Function, Hallucination, and More," Healthline, Last modified Dec. 18, 2018, https://www.healthline.com/health/healthy-sleep/how-long-can-you-go-without-sleep.
3. Vandergriendt, "How Long Can You Go Without Sleep?"
4. Jacob Dubé, "Daylight Savings Time Switch Linked To 28 Fatal Car Accidents in U.S., Study Says," Driving, 2020, https://driving.ca/news/canada/daylight-saving-time-switch-linked-to-28-fatal-car-accidents-in-u-s-study-says.
5. Kirsten Nunez, "The 5 Stages of Sleep Deprivation," Healthline, Last modified May 26, 2020, https://www.healthline.com/health/sleep-deprivation/sleep-deprivation-stages.

14. Know When, Where & Why

1. Denney, *Overdrive*, 63-65.
2. Denney, *Overdrive*, 60-67.
3. "The Balmoral Hotel, where J.K. Rowling finished Harry Potter and the Deathly Hallows," The Rowling Library, Last modified June 1, 2016, https://www.therowlinglibrary.com/2016/06/01/the-balmoral-hotel-where-j-k-rowling-finished-harry-potter-and-the-deathly-hallows/.
4. Denney, *Overdrive*, 81.

15. Support

1. Roberts, *Confessions*, Kindle loc 381.

16. Anticipate Challenges

1. Lewis, "How to Write a Novel in only Ten Days," The Novel Smithy, Last modified Oct. 29, 2019, https://thenovelsmithy.com/write-a-novel-in-ten-days/.
2. Jorstad, "Ten Days."
3. Denney, *Overdrive*, 116.
4. Newport, *Deep Work.* 146-149
5. Alex Pang, *The Distraction Addiction* (Little, Brown and Company, 2013), 187 and 197.

17. End It Productively

1. Jerry Jenkins, "Participating in NaNo Writing 2020? Caution!" Jerry Jenkins, Accessed May 6, 2021, https://jerryjenkins.com/nanowrimo/.

18. How to Stick the Landing

1. Jerry Jenkins, "How to End A Story: 3 Secrets to Writing a Captivating Ending," Jerry Jenkins, Accessed May 6, 2021, https://jerryjenkins.com/how-to-end-a-story/.
2. August Birch, "Writer: Seven Unforgettable Ways to End Your Next Novel," Medium, Last updated September 13, 2018, https://augustbirch.medium.com/seven-unforgettable-ways-to-end-your-next-novel-93020fd24787.
3. Bridget McNulty, "How to end a book: 8 tips for a rewarding read," Now Novel, Accessed May 6, 2021, https://www.nownovel.com/blog/writing-the-end-of-your-novel/.
4. McNulty, "How to end a book."

19. Editing the Three-Day Novel

1. Ian Cannon, "Everything You Need to Know About Editing Novels," 2019, https://www.thisisallcanon.com/blog/everything-you-need-know-about-editing-novels.

2. Cannon, "Editing Novels."

22. Appendix C

1. Mary Ann Tippett, "Recipes," Mary Ann's Book Reviews 2019 https://maryanntippett.ca/all-energy-no-sugar-banana-bread/.

ACKNOWLEDGMENTS

I owe a debt of gratitude to the following people who made this book possible:

Noel Alcoba, Doug Diaczuk, Brenton Dickieson, Geoffreyjen Edwards, Cynthia Gould, Annie Mahoney, and BD Wilson who generously participated in my interviews and emails.

Brenna Bailey-Davies, cherished editor and citation wiz.

Elle Maxwell, who creates covers that capture my vibe.

Sutton Fox and Angelique Bosman, above and beyond beta readers.

Alan Tippett, who agreed to proofreading my final draft and whose attention to detail is unmatched.

ABOUT THE AUTHOR

MARY ANN TIPPETT writes and publishes uplifting fiction. Her high school essays were written at night and last minute. A practice she failed to unlearn in college and law school. She now lives in the capital city of Canada where she blogs about books, shares recipes and insists anything worth doing can be done in three days.

ALSO BY MARY ANN TIPPETT

Finding Clara

The Shape of Us

Pairs With Pinot

www.ingramcontent.com/pod-product-compliance
Lightning Source LLC
Chambersburg PA
CBHW030307100526
44590CB00012B/556